11/13

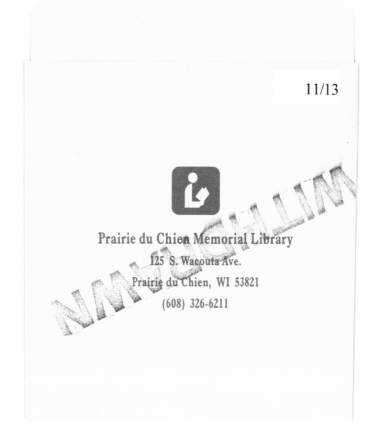

Prairie du Chien Memorial Library
125 S. Wacouta Ave.
Prairie du Chien, WI 53821
(608) 326-6211

THE WORLD CUP

by Alex Monnig

22.95
11/13

Published by ABDO Publishing Company, PO Box 398166, Minneapolis, MN 55439. Copyright © 2013 by Abdo Consulting Group, Inc. International copyrights reserved in all countries. No part of this book may be reproduced in any form without written permission from the publisher. SportsZone™ is a trademark and logo of ABDO Publishing Company.

Printed in the United States of America,
North Mankato, Minnesota
102012
012013

Editor: Chrös McDougall
Series Designer: Craig Hinton

Photo Credits: Carlo Fumagalli/AP Images, cover; Armando Franco/AP Images, title; Jerry Cooke/ Sports Illustrated/Getty Images, 5; AP Images, 9, 12, 17, 21, 23, 24, 31, 33, 43, 58, 59 (top, right), 60 (center); Bettmann/Corbis/AP Images, 15; Agencia Estado/AP Images, 29; STF/AFP/Getty Images, 37, 59 (top, left); Steve Powell/Allsport/Getty Images, 39; Eric Draper/AP Images, 44; Bruno Luca/ AP Images, 47, 54, 56, 59 (bottom); Dusan Vranic/AP Images, 49; Fritz Reiss/AP Images, 60 (top); Strumpf/AP Images, 60 (bottom)

Cataloging-in-Publication Data
Monnig, Alex.
 The World Cup / Alex Monnig.
   p. cm. -- (Sports' great championships)
Includes bibliographical references and index.
ISBN 978-1-61783-675-6
1. Soccer--History--Juvenile literature. 2. World Cup (Soccer)--History--Juvenile literature. I. Title.
796.334/668--dc22

2012946241

TABLE OF CONTENTS

Brazil Brings Back the Trophy

Pelé is a simple name that for many is synonymous with soccer. After all, most people agree that the Brazilian playmaker was one of the best players ever.

In 1970, however, he had not quite earned that legendary status yet. Pelé, whose full name is Edson Arantes do Nascimento, had shown flashes of brilliance. The 1958 World Cup in Sweden was one of those times. Though he was just 17 years old, the forward scored six goals in four games. That helped Brazil win its first World Cup.

Pelé, *third from right*, had won two World Cups with Brazil, but his breakout performance came in 1970 in Mexico.

TV Rules

There were downfalls to the increased television presence at the 1970 World Cup. One was the game times. Many soccer fans wanted to watch the games in Europe. So organizers scheduled the games to kick off during the European evening. That allowed more people to watch. But it also meant the games had to be played under the brutal midday heat of a Mexico summer.

Pelé was soon recognized as the world's best player. Brazil then won the World Cup again in 1962 largely without Pelé. An injury knocked him out of the tournament after just two games. His teammate Garrincha, meanwhile, led Brazil to the title. Pelé was then the victim of a brutal 1966 World Cup. Opposing defenders played Pelé rough. He had to sit out the second game with injuries. Brazil was eliminated before the knockout round when it lost its third match.

The 1970 World Cup in Mexico was Pelé's chance for redemption. He was 29 years old and dealing with leg injuries. But he was about to cement his legacy in soccer history. And he would do it in front of millions of fans who were watching around the world.

Soccer to the Masses

The World Cup started out as a small event. By 1970, it was huge. Fans packed the stadiums. Others around the world tried to watch on television. Those watching the 1970 World Cup on television were treated to something new. It was the first time the games were broadcast in color. It could not have come at a better time.

The Brazilians prided themselves on playing what they called *Jogo Bonito*. That is Portuguese for "the beautiful game." Brazil's style was unlike any other in the world at the time. It was free-flowing and offensive. Players formed miniature moving triangles around the field to pass balls at sharp angles. When not passing, the players displayed great ball skills. The key, though, was possession. Brazil could hold on

A Cautionary Tale

Brazil's fast-paced, possession-oriented game made it hard for opponents. For many, the only way to stop Brazil was to play rough. That was what happened in the 1966 World Cup when Pelé was injured. And since there were no substitutions allowed at the time, injured players were forced to play on. After that, Pelé declared that he would not play in the 1970 World Cup without changes. Nobody wanted another World Cup without the world's best player. So red and yellow cards were introduced for the 1970 World Cup. Plus, teams were allowed to make substitutions.

Pelé

Brazil's most famous soccer player ever was not always known as Pelé. His birth certificate reads Edson Arantes do Nascimento. He was named after Thomas Edison, the US inventor of the light bulb. Pelé's father's name is Dondinho, and he was also a soccer player. So at first, Pelé's parents gave him the nickname of "Dico." He got his more famous nickname from schoolmates. They called him Pelé because he had a habit of pronouncing a local goalkeeper's name incorrectly. Instead of saying "Bile," he would say "Pile." But as his legend grew, he became known by another nickname: "O Rei." That means "The King" in Portuguese, which is the language of Brazil. One of the reasons he got that name was because of his prolific scoring. He netted 77 goals in 91 games for Brazil. The national team went 66–11–14 in games in which he played.

to the ball for what seemed like forever. Opponents could not score if they could not get the ball.

The 1970 World Cup was *Jogo Bonito* at its peak. The Brazilians, in their bright yellow jerseys, passed and dribbled and ran like few had ever seen. And in 1970, they did it in living color for fans around the world to see.

The Games Begin

The 1970 World Cup was expected to be a clash of two powers, Brazil and England. It was also a clash of two different playing styles. Brazil, which had won the 1958 and 1962 World Cups, thrived using its *Jogo*

SUECIA
ÄLKOM

Pelé shoots the ball past Uruguay's goalie during the semifinal of the 1970 World Cup. Brazil led all teams with 19 goals and an average of 3.2 goals per game.

Bonito style. England, which had won the 1966 World Cup, had a more sturdy, gritty approach.

Fans did not have to wait long to see the two teams. In what was known as "the final that could have been," Brazil and England faced off in their second game. Brazil was coming off a strong 4–1 win over Czechoslovakia. England, meanwhile, had grinded out a 1–0 victory over Romania to start the tournament.

Their game proved to be more of an English result. Pelé nearly put Brazil up in the first half. His leaping header bounced toward the corner of England's goal. It looked certain to go in. Then a diving England goalkeeper Gordon Banks met the ball with his right hand. That became one of the most famous saves in World Cup history.

But England could not keep Brazil off the scoreboard forever. In the 59th minute, midfielder Tostão received the ball just outside the top left corner of the penalty area. He beat three English defenders. With his back to the net, he twirled his body around, falling, and sent a slow, arching cross with his right foot.

The ball found Pelé near the center of the box. He settled the ball with his right foot as three defenders ran toward him. They expected the scoring machine to shoot. But Pelé's greatness was not limited to scoring. On this play he slid the ball to his right. It was right in the path of oncoming Brazil forward Jairzinho. Jairzinho fired a shot past Banks to give Brazil the 1–0 lead. That remained the final score.

Wrapping Up a Third Cup

Brazil continued its colorful offensive show after that. Pelé scored twice in the final group match, a 3–2 victory over Romania. Brazil then beat Peru 4–2 in the quarterfinals and Uruguay 3–1 in the semifinals. That set up a final with Italy in Mexico City's Azteca Stadium.

Italy brought its own unique challenge. Like Brazil, Italy was known for its style of play. But unlike Brazil, Italy played a very defensive game. Italy kept extra defenders in its penalty area. That made it harder for Brazil to get the ball in close. Instead the South Americans had to play their *Jogo Bonito* out wide. And that is what they did.

Brazil was awarded a throw-in in the 18th minute. Midfielder Roberto Rivelino looped in a cross toward the middle of the box. Pelé stood just 5-foot-7. Yet he leaped into the air and beat his defender to the ball. With a powerful thrust of his head he sent it past diving Italian goalkeeper Enrico Albertosi. Just like that, Brazil was up 1–0.

Italy was not done, though. Brazil midfielder Clodoaldo was sloppy with the ball in the 36th minute. Italy forward Roberto Boninsegna took control of the ball. Then he moved around Brazil goalkeeper Félix to tie the game at 1–1.

Pelé is carried off the field after leading Brazil to its third World Cup victory in 1970. Through 2010 Brazil had a record five World Cup titles.

That score stuck until the 66th minute. Then Brazilian midfielder Gerson ripped a shot from outside the box with his left foot. It found the corner of the net to give Brazil a 2–1 lead.

Brazil was starting to have its way with the Italian defense. Five minutes later it was Pelé's turn to shine again. He headed the ball down in the box into the path of an oncoming Jairzinho, who scored to increase Brazil's lead to 3–1.

Brazil saved its best goal for last. In the 86th minute Clodoaldo got the ball in his own half. He then beat four Italy players on his own. Then

He Said It

"I told myself before the game, 'He's made of skin and bones just like everybody else.' But I was wrong." —Italy defender Tarcisio Burgnich talking about Brazil star Pelé after the 1970 World Cup final

he passed to Jairzinho on the left side. Jairzinho dribbled into the middle of the field. Then he slid the ball to Pelé. Pelé held on to the ball long enough for right fullback Carlos Alberto to charge down the field. Pelé knocked the ball into his path. Alberto then buried it in the back of the net to seal the 4–1 victory. Brazil sealed its third World Cup title with *Jogo Bonito* at its finest.

The winners had scored 19 goals in six games. They had overcome the crunching tackles of England and the tight defensive structure of Italy. Pelé, with his third World Cup title, was officially a legend.

But the flair and style of *Jogo Bonito* would not always triumph. Throughout the years different teams and tactics succeeded in different sites around the world. And every time, more and more people around the world tuned in.

Creating the Cup

Humans have played soccer-like games for centuries. The modern sport, however, truly began in 1863 in England. That is when a group of English clubs adopted a standard set of rules. Chief among those rules was outlawing the use of hands.

The sport grew rapidly in the following decades. By 1904, people around the world were playing soccer. So the Fédération Internationale de Football Association (FIFA) formed to organize the sport. And before long, FIFA began organizing the World Cup.

Uruguay, *in white*, beat Switzerland to win the 1924 Olympic soccer gold medal. The Olympic Games served as soccer's original world championship.

Kicking Off

FIFA President Jules Rimet first proposed a World Cup in 1928. Since 1908, the Olympic Games had served as soccer's world championship. However, those early Olympics were held in Europe. The soccer tournament ended up being primarily European teams. Then Uruguay came in and won the Olympic title in 1924 and 1928. That South American country would be celebrating its 100th year of independence in 1930. So Rimet suggested it host the first World Cup that year.

Thirteen teams accepted invitations to play in the tournament. England was not one of those teams. The country that created modern soccer felt the World Cup was beneath it. Other European teams had shown interest in playing. However, only Belgium, France, Romania, and Yugoslavia showed up. The 15-day boat ride from Europe proved too far

THE WORLD CUP

Uruguay's massive Centenario Stadium was full for the 1930 World Cup final featuring the home team, but other games had far fewer fans.

for many European nations. European teams that did go trained on the decks of the ships on the way.

The 1930 World Cup was a modest tournament by today's standards. The centerpiece Centenario Stadium in Montevideo was not ready when the tournament started. Even when it did open, crowds were small. A preliminary game between Chile and France drew just 2,000 fans to the 70,000-seat stadium. Fewer than 5,000 fans showed up to the World Cup opener between France and Mexico at a different stadium in Montevideo. France forward Lucien Laurent scored the first goal in tournament history on a 12-yard volley. His team won 4–1.

Interest in the tournament grew with each game. It reached its peak in the final. Hosts Uruguay faced neighboring Argentina. A crowd of

Jules's Jewel

The World Cup trophy is called the Jules Rimet Cup. French sculptor Abel Lafleur created the first trophy. It was a 35-centimeter (13.8-inch) statue of Nike, the Greek goddess of victory. It weighed nearly 4 kilograms (8.8 pounds). A new trophy was made in 1983 after the original was stolen.

80,000 fans watched at Centenario Stadium as Uruguay won 4–2. The World Cup was on its way.

Back for More

By 1934, 32 teams wanted to take part in the second World Cup. A qualifying round determined 16 finalists who competed for the title in Italy. Still, it was not quite a *world* tournament yet. Powerful England once again refused to participate. So did defending champion Uruguay. It refused to show up after so many European countries skipped the first World Cup. One team that did make the trip was Egypt. Now countries from Africa, Europe, North America, and South America were represented.

Other aspects of the tournament grew as well. All of the 1930 games were held in one city. Eight different cities hosted games in Italy in 1934. However, fans did not have to travel to be close to the action. That is because the tournament was broadcast on radio to 12 of the 16 countries taking part.

There was a dark cloud over the 1934 World Cup, though. Italy dictator Benito Mussolini hoped to use the tournament for political gain. He thought the unity and success of the Italian team would be a good symbol for his fascist government.

Italy indeed had success. It reached the final against Czechoslovakia. The two European teams played to a 1–1 tie through 90 minutes. So the 1934 final became the first to feature extra time. Approximately seven minutes in, Italy midfielder Giuseppe Meazza found forward Angelo Schiavo for the winning goal. Once again, the host country had won.

Pelé's Predecessor

Most people agree that Pelé was the best Brazilian soccer player ever. But forward Leónidas da Silva helped pave the way. Leónidas was known as "El Diamante Negro" (The Black Diamond) and "The Rubber Man," because he was so acrobatic. His most lasting legacy was inventing the bicycle kick. That is when a player jumps in the air and flips over, kicking the ball while he is upside-down.

Silva scored Brazil's only goal in the 1934 World Cup. Then he broke out in France in 1938. Silva won the Golden Boot as the tournament's top goal-scorer. He might have scored more, but Brazil's coach left him out of the semifinal. The coach wanted Silva to be fresh for the final. Instead, Brazil lost 2–1 to defending champion Italy in the semifinal.

Before the War

World War II was brewing on the horizon in the late 1930s. Still, FIFA decided to go ahead with the 1938 World Cup in France. This angered South American teams. They wanted the tournament to return to their continent. Only Brazil ended up making the trip from South America. However, the Dutch East Indies (now Indonesia) became the World Cup's first Asian participant.

Italy, known as the *Azzurri,* or the Blues, won the tournament again. Meazza had three assists in Italy's 4–2 win over Hungary in the final. But Italy had to go to extreme measures to hold on to the trophy.

World War II escalated in Europe in 1939. There was concern that Mussolini and his Nazi allies would try to steal the Jules Rimet Cup. So an Italian vice president of FIFA hid the trophy in a shoebox under his bed until the war was over. The war raged in Europe and Asia until 1945. That forced FIFA to cancel both the 1942 and 1946 World Cups. It was a hard time for international soccer. The first three World Cups had been overshadowed by politics and boycotts. Now fans would have to wait 12 years for another one.

Hungary goalkeeper Antal Szabo reaches to stop a shot by Italy's Silvio Piola during the 1938 World Cup final in Paris, France.

Soccer Spreads

F ew Americans even knew a US team had traveled to Brazil for the 1950 World Cup. And few expected much from the team after a 3–1 loss to Spain in the opener. Powerhouse England, finally playing in its first World Cup, was up next. "If Spain scored three on us, England was going to run right over us," US defender Harry Keough said.

England indeed dominated. But the game's only goal came from US forward Joe Gaetjens in the 37th minute. US midfielder Walter Bahr shot the ball. Then Gaetjens dove through traffic and redirected it into the net.

Fans carry US forward Joe Gaetjens off the field after his goal secured one of soccer's greatest upsets when the United States beat England in the 1950 World Cup.

Brazil's Francisco Aramburu, *in white*, heads the ball toward Uruguay goalie Roque Maspoli in the 1950 World Cup final. It did not go in, however, and Uruguay won 2–1.

Brazilian fans carried Gaetjens off the field afterward to celebrate one of the biggest upsets in World Cup history: USA 1, England 0.

Neither England nor the United States did much else in Brazil. Both teams were eliminated after the group stage. In the aftermath of World War II, only 13 teams took part in the 1950 World Cup. Defeated nations Germany and Japan were barred. That opened the door for Brazil to win its first World Cup.

Soccer had taken off in Brazil after its team reached the 1938 semifinals. Brazilians wanted to show the world just how committed they were to the World Cup in 1950. So they built the giant Maracanã stadium in the capital city of Rio de Janeiro. It held an amazing 200,000 people.

The odd number of teams led to a unique format. The final round consisted of a four-team round robin. Teams earned two points for a win and one for a tie. Whoever ended with the most was world champion.

The tournament came down to a match between the host Brazilians and neighboring Uruguay in the Maracanã. All Brazil needed to do was tie. The hosts were confident. They were presented with gold watches for winning before the match even started. A Brazilian newspaper even ran an early story declaring Brazil champions.

The stadium was packed with fans. They cheered as forward Friaca put Brazil up 1–0 in the 47th minute. Victory was so close. Or was it? Uruguay forward Juan Schiaffino tied the game in the 66th minute. Then Uruguay forward Ghiggia put his team ahead with eleven minutes remaining. Ghiggia beat Brazil goalie Barbosa to the short side. Uruguay held on to stun Brazil 2–1 and capture a second World Cup.

Shocks and Scores in Switzerland

The World Cup returned to Europe in 1954 when Switzerland hosted. Though few had the ability to watch, the 1954 World Cup was the first to be broadcast on television. Meanwhile, South Korea became the second Asian country to take part in the tournament. Of the 16 participants, though, Hungary was the team to beat.

Hungary was a new soccer superpower. It had won gold at the 1952 Olympic Games. The team had not lost in four years. It appeared inevitable that the "Mighty Magyars" would win again in Switzerland.

And they did win a lot of games. Hungary won its two group-stage games by a combined 17–3. Then it beat Brazil 4–2 in the quarterfinals. That game became known as "The Battle of Bern." Players and coaches fought each other during and after the game in Bern, Switzerland.

After Hungary's 4–2 extra-time victory over Uruguay in the semifinals, the Magyars played in "The Miracle of Bern." Only the miracle that rainy night in Bern was not on Hungary's side.

The Magyars stormed out to a 2–0 lead over West Germany in the first eight minutes. They had already beaten West Germany 8–3 in the group stage. A win appeared inevitable. But the Germans came back to score twice in the next 10 minutes.

Hungary had several chances to take the lead back but could not. Finally, with less than six minutes to go, West Germany's Helmut Rahn put his team up for good, 3–2. The Magyars had missed their chance.

Breathtaking Brazil

Brazil had come agonizingly close to winning the World Cup at home in 1950. By 1958, Brazil was established as a strong soccer country. But to that point, Uruguay was clearly the most successful South American country. After all, it had two World Cup titles to Brazil's zero.

Pelé and Brazil changed that with an incredible stretch beginning at the 1958 World Cup in Sweden. The 17-year-old Pelé notched six goals in four matches. He became the youngest goal scorer in World Cup

Goals Galore

The 1954 World Cup in Switzerland featured 140 goals scored. That was more than five per game—the most ever in a World Cup through 2010. Twelve of them came in one match. Austria defeated Switzerland 7–5 in the quarterfinals. Through 2010 it was the highest scoring World Cup game ever. However, three teams—Czechoslovakia, South Korea, and Scotland—did not manage to score any goals.

Just Does It

Pelé and his Brazilian teammates wowed the world with their *Jogo Bonito* on the way to winning their first World Cup. But they were not the only stars of the 1958 show in Sweden. France forward Just Fontaine scored 13 goals during the tournament. That set a record that still had not been broken through the 2010 World Cup. He netted six in France's group matches—all wins—against Paraguay, Yugoslavia, and Scotland. He followed that up with two in the quarterfinal victory against Northern Ireland and one in France's semifinal loss to Brazil. But he saved his best for last. He tallied four goals in France's triumph in the third-place match against West Germany. Surprisingly, he was only added to France's World Cup team as an injury replacement. He even forgot to bring his shoes, so he had to borrow some from teammate Stéphane Bruey.

history. In the semifinals, Brazil outscored France and its high-flying forward Just Fontaine 5–2. Then it beat host Sweden by the same score in the final.

An earthquake in host country Chile two years earlier nearly delayed the 1962 World Cup. But the country rallied around the event. Roads and buildings were fixed up so Chile could show everyone just what it had to offer. Brutal play on the field marred the tournament. A group-stage game between Italy and Chile became known as "The Battle of Santiago."

Pelé went out early because of injuries as well. But Brazil forward Garrincha led the squad around the field. He had a part in most of Brazil's goals.

Brazil forward Garrincha, *left*, stepped up in Pelé's absence to lead Brazil to the 1962 World Cup title in Chile. It was Brazil's second of the five titles through 2010.

The veteran team, which included nine players from the 1958 triumph in Sweden, used just 12 players in its march to a second consecutive title. The team's exciting, offensive soccer triumphed over the rough, defensive game most countries played. Only Italy had previously won back-to-back World Cups. And only Italy and Uruguay had won two World Cups. A new global soccer power had emerged.

Scintillating Soccer

England was the place where soccer had truly taken off in the 1800s. Soccer would take off again when the 1966 World Cup was held there. For the first time, games were broadcast live to all of Europe. There was also an official mascot for the first time. Items with World Cup Willie were sold all over England. The lion mascot was such a hit that FIFA decided there should be one for every World Cup.

Brazil came in as the favorite to win its third World Cup in a row. But Pelé was injured again. This time he was the victim of very physical play

Portugal forward Eusébio scored nine goals to win the Golden Boot at the 1966 World Cup. He led his team to a third-place finish.

from Bulgaria's defenders in the opening game. Without Pelé, Brazil failed to advance to the knockout stage.

"The Shock of the Century"

North Korea was a team of small players from a small country. It was not expected to go very far in the 1966 World Cup. But on July 19 in Ayersome Park in Middlesbrough, it pulled one of the biggest upsets in tournament history. North Korea took out heavyweights Italy 1–0.

Midfielder Pak Doo Ik scored to put North Korea ahead in the 42nd minute. Italy was unable to come back and was eliminated after the group stage. North Korea then went on to play Portugal in the quarterfinals. For a while it looked like it would pull another upset. North Korea stormed out to a 3–0 lead in the first 25 minutes. But Portugal's star forward Eusébio scored four times in his team's 5–3 comeback victory.

England, meanwhile, cruised through the first round. Then forward Bobby Charlton and defender and captain Bobby Moore led the hosts past Argentina 1–0 in the quarterfinals. Now two elite teams and two elite players stood in England's path to a World Cup title.

First up were Eusébio and Portugal. The young forward nicknamed "The Black Panther" scored nine goals in the 1966 World Cup to win the Golden Boot Award. However, only one of those goals came against England. Eusébio's 82nd-minute

penalty kick goal was not enough. Charlton scored twice to give England the 2–1 win.

Next up were West Germany and its game-changing defender Franz Beckenbauer in the final. Beckenbauer revolutionized the sweeper position in central defense. He could also score. The 20-year-old notched four goals during the World Cup.

Approximately 400 million television viewers tuned in to the final from Wembley Stadium in London. They watched as the two teams traded goals in the first 18 minutes. They watched as England took the lead in the 78th. Then they watched as West Germany's Wolfgang Weber tied it in the 89th.

However, England was at its strongest when the game went to extra time. Forward Geoff Hurst scored twice to give his country a 4–2 victory. Hurst had also scored England's first goal. After a rocky early relationship with the international soccer community, the creators were finally on top.

Total Voetbal Comes up Short

Pelé wrapped up his storied international career with a third World Cup title for Brazil in 1970. That made Brazil the most successful country with three World Cup wins. And Brazil did it by playing with flair.

Morocco Makes It

In 1970, Morocco became the first African team to make the tournament since Egypt in 1934. One reason Morocco was able to take part was because African nations were given an easier path to qualify. In the past African teams had to beat teams from other continents. In 1970 Morocco only had to beat other African teams. The World Cup has included at least one African team ever since.

In 1974, *Jogo Bonito* was overshadowed by *Total Voetbal*. That is Dutch for "Total Football." Holland adopted its system from a Dutch club team called Ajax. Total Football was an open, exciting style of football—much like *Jogo Bonito*. But it was also very tactical. The players were free to move around the field and switch positions at will. They had to be both smart and skilled.

Holland had a perfect leader in forward Johan Cruyff. He was already known as one of the best players in Europe. At the 1974 World Cup in Germany, he proved himself to the world. Along with midfielder Johan Neeskens, Cruyff led Holland straight to the final. The team in the bright orange jerseys surprised some opponents. The opponents did not know where the attack was going to come from. The result was 14 goals scored with only one allowed in six games leading up to the final.

Beckenbauer and host West Germany were the last ones who could stop Total Football. That did not appear likely, though. Holland opened with a series of passes and took a 1–0 lead on a penalty kick before West Germany even touched the ball. But West Germany came back.

A penalty kick tied the game 1–1 in the 25th minute. Then forward Gerd Mueller put the hosts up 2–1 just before halftime. The clinical West German defense shut down Cruyff and the rest of Holland to preserve the victory.

Holland remained a world-class team into the 1978 World Cup in Argentina. But they had to play without Cruyff. The Dutch star skipped the tournament in protest of General Jorge Rafael Videla, who had used his military group to take over Argentina. Fears of potential violence and match fixing nearly overshadowed the tournament.

Dutch midfielder Johann Cruyff (14) epitomized the successful "Total Football" philosophy. However, Holland fell short of a World Cup during the 1970s.

Ultimately Holland was able to make it back to the final against Argentina. Like the Magical Magyars from Hungary, however, the Total Football era from Holland never produced a World Cup title. Argentina won 3–1 after extra time. After losing again in the 2010 final, Holland was still looking for its first World Cup.

Bigger and Better

By 1982, FIFA had started accepting smaller countries into its organization. That meant more teams were trying to qualify for the World Cup. Meanwhile, more and more fans around the world were watching the games. That meant more opportunities for advertisers at the World Cup. As more companies paid to be affiliated with the tournament, the World Cup continued to grow into the global behemoth it is today.

The 1982 World Cup in Spain was the first to include 24 teams. It was a disappointing showing for defending champion Argentina. The team

Italy's Claudio Gentile (6) and Dino Zoff (1) hold the World Cup Trophy after defeating West Germany in the 1982 World Cup final in Madrid, Spain.

failed to reach the semifinals. Meanwhile, 21-year-old midfield phenom Diego Maradona was sent off with a red card in a second-round loss. The feisty Maradona kicked a Brazilian player. He would soon be back in a big way, though.

Italy appeared to be on its way out of the tournament early as well. It tied its first three games. Star forward Paolo Rossi did not score in any of those games. He was just returning to the team after a two-year ban for being involved with a cheating scandal. But Rossi came alive after that. He scored six times in the team's final three games. He capped off his Golden Boot performance in the final against West Germany. Rossi scored the opening goal in Italy's 3–1 victory. The Italians had matched Brazil with three World Cup titles.

Marvelous Maradona

The 1982 World Cup was forgettable for Maradona and Argentina fans. What Maradona did in 1986 in Mexico, however, still has fans around the world talking. The Argentina captain was everywhere on the field. He scored five goals and assisted on five more in Argentina's seven games. And two goals he scored against England in the quarterfinals went down in World Cup history.

The first was early in the second half. Maradona charged with the ball toward the England penalty box. He slipped the ball to a teammate to his right. But England midfielder Steve Hodge got his foot to it. The ball slowly floated toward England goalkeeper Peter Shilton. Maradona was

Platini's Performances

One of the greatest players of the 1980s never won a World Cup. France midfielder Michel Platini was one of the game's best playmakers. He brought his *Les Bleus* to the World Cup semifinals in 1982 and 1986. They never got beyond that, though. Those exciting French teams earned the nickname the "Brazilians of Europe." Platini later went on to become a top soccer administrator in Europe.

not going to let Shilton casually catch it. The 5-foot-5 Maradona charged at Shilton and tried to outjump the 6-foot-1 goalie.

Maradona indeed touched the ball first. But the contact was with his left hand. The ball then bounced into the net. Shilton and other England players immediately signaled for a hand ball. But the referees let the goal stand. Nobody knows if Maradona's hand ball was on purpose. But the goal forever became known as "The Hand of God" goal.

If the first goal was controversial, the second goal was pure ability. A few minutes after the disputed goal, Maradona gathered the ball in his own half. He spun away from two defenders and sprinted down the right sideline. Then he cut back toward the goal and dribbled past two more defenders. As Maradona entered the box, Shilton charged at him. But Maradona dribbled around the goalie. He slid the ball into the net just before being taken out by a tackle.

"The second goal was, and still is, the best goal ever scored," said Gary Lineker, England striker and winner of the 1986 Golden Boot. "To do what he did was just extraordinary. I have to say I just stood there on the halfway line and thought 'Wow.'"

Maradona and Argentina kept rolling after that 2–1 victory. Maradona scored two more goals in a 2–0 win over Belgium in the semifinals. Then he drew so much attention from the West Germany defense in the final

Argentina's Diego Maradona leaps over two West German defenders during the 1986 World Cup final in Mexico City, Mexico.

that his teammates had room to shine. Argentina won 3–2 and took home its second World Cup title.

Slow and Steady

In 1986, Maradona scored five goals on the way to the championship. At the 1990 World Cup in Italy, Argentina scored five total goals. But that proved to be enough to reach the final, where it played West Germany.

Approximately 26 billion people watched on television. But those low scores were the story in Italy. The 2.21 goals per game were the lowest of any World Cup through 2010. The low scores resulted in many games going to extra time and shootouts, including both semifinals.

US forward Eric Wynalda (11) heads the ball past two Colombia defenders during a group-stage game at the 1994 World Cup.

In the final, the slower, defensive play favored West Germany. The team no longer had Franz Beckenbauer anchoring its back line. But it did have Beckenbauer on the sideline as manager. And his West German defense stood strong against Argentina. Andreas Brehme scored the game's only goal in the 85th minute to give West Germany a 1–0 win. That capped off a stretch in which that country reached the World Cup final four times in five tournaments. West Germany won two of those.

Coming to America

The United States had competed in the 1930 and 1950 World Cups. However, soccer fell into the background. Other sports such as baseball and football took most of the attention. Still, FIFA saw great potential in the United States. So in 1988 it awarded the 1994 World Cup to the young soccer country.

In many ways, the 1994 World Cup was a huge success. More than 3.5 million people packed the stadiums. The World Cup expanded from 24 to 32 teams beginning in 1998. Yet through 2010, no World Cup had drawn more fans than 1994. And those fans saw a lot of goals. The 141 goals scored in 1994 were the most since the 146 scored in 1982 in Spain.

Heavyweights: Out

Several emerging countries made exciting runs at the 1994 World Cup. Behind star forward Hristo Stoichkov, Bulgaria reached the semifinals. Meanwhile, Romania reached the quarterfinals, and Nigeria, Saudi Arabia, and the United States all reached the round of 16. And two traditional soccer heavyweights missed out. England failed to qualify four years after finishing fourth in Italy. France missed its second World Cup in a row. And Argentina played most of the tournament without Diego Maradona. After the team's second game, the star was taken for a routine random drug test. The test showed he had a banned substance called ephedrine in his system. Maradona was suspended 18 months, ending his international career.

Hometown fans had something extra to cheer about. The United States had narrowly qualified for the 1990 World Cup in Italy. But it lost all three games. In 1994, the United States tied Switzerland and beat Colombia in the first round. That clinched a second-round date with Brazil.

Colombia Killing

People in some countries treat sports very seriously. Fans can become very attached to teams. Sometimes that leads to violence. In 1994, it even meant the death of a player.

Colombia came into the 1994 World Cup as a favorite. Pelé even picked it to finish in the top four. But a 2–1 loss to the United States eliminated Colombia in the group stage. Colombia defender Andrés Escobar was responsible for one of the goals. He accidentally hit the ball into his own net. Colombians were furious. Escobar received numerous death threats upon returning home.

On July 2, Escobar was killed while exiting a nightclub in Medellín, Colombia. The killer yelled "Goal!" as he fired his gun. More than 120,000 people attended the funeral for Escobar. He was often called "The Gentleman of Football."

The dream run ended there. Brazil beat the United States 1–0 in front of 84,147 fans at Stanford Stadium near San Francisco. Behind prolific forward Romario, Brazil continued all the way to the final. Romario scored or assisted 10 of Brazil's 11 goals in the tournament. Brazil met another star striker in the final. Italy's Roberto Baggio had scored five goals in three knockout-round games.

Yet nobody on either team could find the net in the final. The 94,194 fans at the Rose Bowl in Pasadena, California, watched 90 minutes of regulation and 30 minutes of extra time without a goal. So it became the first World Cup final to be decided by penalty kicks.

Brazil star forward Romario, *right*, and Italy star defender Paolo Maldini, *left*, battle for the ball during the 1994 World Cup final in Pasadena, California.

Brazil had a 3–2 lead when Baggio stepped forward to take Italy's fifth and final shot. A goal would tie the game and move the shootout into sudden death. A miss meant a Brazil win. Italy fans had to feel good about their chances. Baggio was one of the world's most lethal goal scorers. But when he drilled a shot with his right foot, the ball sailed over the crossbar.

With the legendary Pelé watching in the stands, Brazil won its record fourth World Cup title. The World Cup was growing to include more and more people in more and more countries. Yet the global powers remained on top.

Ever Expanding

The 1998 World Cup was held in France. A golden generation of French players emerged right in time.

The French roster included standouts such as goalie Fabien Barthez, defenders Marcel Desailly and Lilian Thuram, and midfielders Didier Deschamps and Emmanuel Petit. Three players 21 or younger—forwards Thierry Henry and David Trezeguet and midfielder Patrick Vieira—would go on to be counted among the world's best players. But the true

France midfielder Zinedine Zidane led a golden generation of French players to the World Cup title on home soil in 1998.

superstar was Zinedine Zidane. The attacking midfielder was known for his creativity and playmaking.

Zidane and France quickly began navigating through the first World Cup to include 32 teams. They were not truly tested until the second round. France needed a "golden goal" by defender Laurent Blanc to beat Paraguay 1–0 in extra time. In the quarterfinals, Blanc scored the winning penalty kick to beat Italy 4–3 in a shootout.

First-time World Cup participant Croatia awaited in the semifinals. And star forward Davor Suker put his team up 1–0 in the 46th minute. But Thuram answered one minute later and sealed France's 2–1 victory in the 70th minute. France was headed to its first World Cup final.

The final against Brazil was much anticipated. Brazil forward Ronaldo was known as one of the most prolific goal-scorers of all time. Many Brazil fans were very confident. But questions came out about Ronaldo's health.

Brazil weighed whether or not to include him in the starting lineup. The team ultimately decided to stick with Ronaldo. But he did not play well, and Brazil could not keep up with France.

Zidane opened the scoring in the 27th minute. He rose above Brazilian defenders to head the ball into the net off a corner kick. Then he did it again on another corner kick just before halftime. Petit laid in one final goal in injury time to give France a 3–0 victory. The golden generation of *Les Bleus* had come through.

Eastern Evolution

The World Cup moved to Asia for the first time in 2002 when Japan and South Korea co-hosted. And like in 1994, emerging teams stole the show early on. Senegal opened the tournament by defeating defending champion France 1–0. The United States had a breakout tournament,

Ronaldo's Record

Brazil made it to the finals in two of the three World Cups in which Ronaldo played from 1998 to 2006. It finished on top in 2002. He was a big reason why. In those three tournaments he scored 15 goals. That record still stood through 2010.

reaching the quarterfinals behind the likes of forward Brian McBride, midfielder Claudio Reyna, and goalie Brad Friedel.

The biggest surprises came from South Korea and Turkey. Turkey had not played in a World Cup since 1954. South Korea had not gotten out of the first round in its five World Cup appearances. Yet in 2002, both teams reached the semifinals. On the way, South Korea eliminated powers Italy and Spain. Turkey knocked out Japan and Senegal.

The World Cup final ended up being two traditional powers: Germany and Brazil. Ronaldo and Brazil made up for the disappointing 1998 final. He scored both goals in Brazil's 2–0 win. Through 2010, no country could match Brazil's five World Cup titles.

Zidane Loses His Head

The World Cup returned to Europe in 2006 when Germany hosted. And European teams quickly took control. Ten of the final 16 teams were European. Only Brazil and Argentina survived as non-European teams in the quarterfinals. But France knocked out Brazil and Germany knocked out Argentina. The result was the first all-European semifinals since 1982.

In the end it came down to Italy and France. Defender Fabio Cannavaro and goalie Gianluigi Buffon anchored a dominant Italy defense throughout the tournament. It gave up only one goal on the way to the final. That was in a 1–1 group-stage match against the United States.

France, meanwhile, stumbled early on. It barely reached the knockout round with a win and two draws in the group stage. But then something

"The Battle of Nuremberg"

There had already been "The Battle of Bern" and "The Battle of Santiago." Portugal and Holland's match in Nuremberg, Germany, in the 2006 World Cup might have them both beat. Referee Valentin Ivanov gave out 16 cards. Four of them were red.

It all started with two hard tackles on Portugal star forward Cristiano Ronaldo. Both earned yellow cards. The second forced Ronaldo off in the 34th minute. The flood of cards was opened. Both teams faked injuries and flopped on the ground to draw penalties on the other team. "[The Portuguese] are known for time-wasting or hitting from behind," Ivanov said. "But I was unpleasantly surprised to see such things from the Dutch. What's more, the Dutch were the instigators."

changed. Zidane was playing in his final World Cup. He took his game to another level in the knockout round and led France to the final.

Zidane's storied career appeared ready to end on a high note. In the final, the midfield maestro converted a penalty kick in the seventh minute to put his team ahead. Italy defender Marco Materazzi tied the game 12 minutes later. But neither team scored after that.

A shootout seemed inevitable as the teams grinded through extra time. Then things fell apart for the French. In the 110th minute, Materazzi insulted Zidane's sister. The Frenchman was furious. He turned and head-butted Materazzi right in the chest. Materazzi fell to the ground. The referee immediately ran over and showed Zidane a red card.

"He leaves football in disgrace," the television announcer said as Zidane walked off the field.

A few minutes later the game indeed went to penalty kicks. Italy made all five of its shots against the aging Barthez. Meanwhile, Trezeguet hit the crossbar while shooting second for France. Trezeguet likely would have taken the shot even if Zidane had been available. Still, many people blamed Zidane. Zidane later won the Golden Ball as the tournament's best player. But the head-butt forever tarnished his final game. Italy, meanwhile, celebrated its fourth World Cup title.

Another Venue, Another Spectacle

In 2010, the World Cup could truly be considered global. That year South Africa became the first African nation to host a World Cup. Locals took great pride. They brought lots of energy and excitement into the stands for each game. One way they did that was through vuvuzelas. The buzzing sound from those horns could often be heard throughout entire matches.

The surprise of the tournament came from the original World Cup power. Forwards Luis Suarez and Diego Forlan led Uruguay on a dream run to the semifinals. Forlan, with his long blond hair, became the

Spain's Andrés Iniesta drills home the game-winning goal at the 2010 World Cup final in Johannesburg, South Africa.

tournament's star. He tied for the lead with five goals and won the Golden Ball.

The final, however, was a battle between two European powers that had never won a World Cup. The Netherlands had come so close in the Total Football era of the 1970s. Spain often had some of the best players in the world. But it had never finished better than fourth. Something had to give in the final.

Spain dominated games with its "tiki-taka" style of play. Through a series of small, quick passes, Spain maintained control of the ball. The main maestros were midfielders Xavi and Andrés Iniesta.

For two teams known for appealing play, it was a surprisingly ugly game. A World Cup final-record 14 yellow cards were given out. Nine went to Holland. It took extra time to determine which country would win its first World Cup. Finally, Iniesta drilled a volley from just outside the six-yard box in the 116th minute. Holland's goalie hardly had a chance. The Spanish players poured onto the field in celebration. Four minutes later, it became official. After years of disappointments, Spain had finally won.

The World Cup began as a simple idea in Jules Rimet's head. Today it is a global event. In 2010, an estimated 700 million people watched the World Cup final on television. The tournament has become more than a world championship. It is now a quadrennial world celebration.

TIMELINE

FIFA President Jules Rimet proposes the idea of a World Cup tournament at a FIFA meeting on May 28.

1928

Host Uruguay defeats Argentina 4–2 on July 30 in Centenario Stadium in Montevideo to capture the first World Cup.

1930

World War II causes the cancellation of two tournaments.

1942–46

On June 29, the United States pulls off one of the biggest upsets in World Cup history by stunning England 1–0 on Joe Gaetjens's goal.

1950

Uruguay upsets host Brazil 2–1 to win the World Cup after local media and politicians had already crowned Brazil as champion before kickoff.

1950

Forward Paolo Rossi leads Italy to its third World Cup title, defeating West Germany 3–1 in the final.

1982

On December 20, thieves steal the Jules Rimet Cup from the Brazilian Football Confederation headquarters in Rio de Janeiro. It is never seen again.

1983

Argentina midfielder Diego Maradona scores two famous goals to help his team defeat England 2–1 in the quarterfinals. Argentina later wins the title.

1986

Franz Beckenbauer becomes the first person to win the World Cup as a player and a manager as West Germany defeats Argentina 1–0 in the final.

1990

Colombia defender Andrés Escobar is murdered on July 2 in his home country 10 days after accidentally scoring an own goal in a match against the United States.

1994

1954

Austria beats host Switzerland 7–5 on June 26 in the highest-scoring match in World Cup history through 2010. West Germany wins its first World Cup.

1966

North Korea stuns Italy 1–0 on July 19 in "The Shock of the Century." North Korea goes on to lose to Portugal in the quarterfinals, and England wins the tournament.

1970

Fans around the world are able to watch Pelé and his Brazilian teammates in color for the first time as they capture the World Cup in Mexico.

1974

Led by forward Johan Cruyff, Holland showcases its "Total Football" strategy but falls to West Germany 2–1 in the final.

1978

In its first World Cup game, Tunisia beats Mexico 3–1 on June 2 for the first win by an African country in the tournament. Argentina wins the title.

1994

On July 17, Italy loses to Brazil in the first World Cup final to be decided in a shootout.

1998

France hosts and wins the first World Cup to feature 32 teams.

2002

On May 31, Senegal defeats France 1–0 in Seoul, South Korea. It is the first game of the first World Cup held in Asia.

2006

On July 9, France midfielder Zinedine Zidane is sent off after head-butting Italy defender Marco Materazzi in the World Cup final. Italy wins on penalty kicks.

2010

The World Cup kicks off on June 11 in South Africa. It is the first time an African country hosts the event. Spain beats Holland in the final.

CHAMPIONSHIP OVERVIEW

The Trophy

The first World Cup trophy was the Jules Rimet Cup. It was used until 1970 and was later stolen.

For the 1974 World Cup a new trophy, featuring a soccer ball being held up by several hands, was created.

The Legends

Franz Beckenbauer (West Germany): A World Cup champion as a player (1974) and manager (1990). He also competed in the 1966 and 1970 tournaments.

Diego Maradona (Argentina): Won the Golden Ball in leading his team to 1986 championship. Also competed in 1982, 1990, and 1994 tournaments.

Pelé (Brazil): Helped his team to four World Cups between 1958 and 1970, winning three of them.

Ronaldo (Brazil): Competed in three World Cups between 1998 and 2006. Won the 2002 World Cup, the 1998 Golden Ball, and 2002 Golden Boot.

Zinedine Zidane (France): Led his team to three World Cups from 1998 to 2006, including the 1998 title. Claimed 2006 Golden Ball.

The Victors

Brazil: Five championships (1958, 1962, 1970, 1994, 2002)

Italy: Four (1934, 1938, 1982, 2006)

West Germany/Germany: Three (1954, 1974, 1990)

GLOSSARY

amateur
A player who is not paid to play.

boycotts
When groups of people refuse to do something in protest.

controversy
When there is doubt about the true intention of an action.

dictator
A person that rules over a country without allowing citizens to voice their opinions and make changes in the government.

extra time
Two 15-minute periods added to an elimination game if the score is tied after regulation.

injury time
Time added to the end of each half, as determined by the referee, to account for stoppages in play.

match fixing
Losing a match on purpose.

scandal
A disgraceful incident.

sent off
When a player is ejected from a game due to a red card or two yellow cards.

tactics
Overall plans and strategies used in games.

volley
When a player kicks the ball while it is in the air.

FOR MORE INFORMATION

Selected Bibliography

Crouch, Terry. *The World Cup: The Complete History.* London, England. Aurum Press, 2006.

Fiore, Fernando. *The World Cup.* New York. Harper Collins, 2006.

Hirshey, David and Bennett, Roger. *The ESPN World Cup Companion.* New York: Ballantine Books, 2010.

Further Readings

Black, Alan and Sterry, David Henry. *The Glorious World Cup: A Fanatic's Guide.* New York. New American Library, 2010.

Carlisle, Jeff. *Soccer's Most Wanted II.* Washington, D.C. Potomac Books, 2009.

Christopher, Matt. *World Cup.* New York. Hachette Book Group, 2010.

Hunt, Chris. *World Cup of Soccer: The Complete Guide.* Richmond Hill, Ontario. Firefly Books, 2010.

McDougall, Chrös. *Soccer.* Minneapolis, MN: ABDO Publishing Co. 2012.

Web Links

To learn more about the World Cup, visit ABDO Publishing Company online at **www.abdopublishing.com**. Web sites about the World Cup are featured on our Book Links page. These links are routinely monitored and updated to provide the most current information available.

Places to Visit

National Football Museum
Urbis Building, Cathedral Gardens
Manchester, M4 3BG
+44 (0)161 870 9275
www.nationalfootballmuseum.com
This museum brings to life the history and gameplay of soccer through various interactive exhibits. Admission is free.

Rose Bowl
1001 Rose Bowl Drive
Pasadena, CA 91103
(626) 577-3101
www.rosebowlstadium.com
The 90,000-plus-seat stadium was host to the 1994 World Cup final between Brazil and Italy. It continues to host soccer games on occasion, but is used primarily for football.

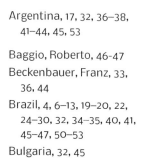

INDEX

About the Author

Alex Monnig is a freelance journalist from St. Louis, Missouri. He got his master's degree from the University of Missouri in May 2010. During his career he has spent time covering sporting events around the world, including the 2008 Olympic Games in China, the 2010 Commonwealth Games in India, and the 2011 Rugby World Cup in New Zealand.